THE INDIAN RIVER GANGES

A CULTURAL AND SPIRITUAL EXPLORATION OF THE RIVER GANGES

DR. JAGADEESH PILLAI

Copyright © Dr. Jagadeesh Pillai
All Rights Reserved.

This book has been self-published with all reasonable efforts taken to make the material error-free by the author. No part of this book shall be used, reproduced in any manner whatsoever without written permission from the author, except in the case of brief quotations embodied in critical articles and reviews.

The Author of this book is solely responsible and liable for its content including but not limited to the views, representations, descriptions, statements, information, opinions and references ["Content"]. The Content of this book shall not constitute or be construed or deemed to reflect the opinion or expression of the Publisher or Editor. Neither the Publisher nor Editor endorse or approve the Content of this book or guarantee the reliability, accuracy or completeness of the Content published herein and do not make any representations or warranties of any kind, express or implied, including but not limited to the implied warranties of merchantability, fitness for a particular purpose. The Publisher and Editor shall not be liable whatsoever for any errors, omissions, whether such errors or omissions result from negligence, accident, or any other cause or claims for loss or damages of any kind, including without limitation, indirect or consequential loss or damage arising out of use, inability to use, or about the reliability, accuracy or sufficiency of the information contained in this book.

Made with ♥ on the Notion Press Platform
www.notionpress.com

|| "Dedicated to all who seek to understand and appreciate Indian culture and tradition." ||

Contents

Contents

Prayer

Ganga Taranga RamaniYAA JatakaLApam

GowRI nirantara vibushitha VAma bagam

Narayana Priya mananga maDApaharam

Vaaranasi Purapathim bhaja Vishwanatham

About The Author

Dr. Jagadeesh Pillai is a renowned Guinness World Record holder, writer, and researcher hailing from Varanasi, also known as the abode of Lord Shiva. With a Ph.D. in Vedic Science and a range of creative ideas and achievements, he is a true polymath. He is the author of more than 100 books including Research Publications. Although his roots can be traced back to Kerala, the people of Varanasi hold him in high regard and affectionately consider him one of their own.

Dr. Pillai has achieved four Guinness World Records in the following subjects:

"Script to Screen" - In this record, Dr. Pillai produced and directed an animation film within the shortest time possible, breaking the previous record set by Canadians. He has also received numerous national and international awards and recognitions for this achievement.

Longest Line of Postcards - For this record, Dr. Pillai created a line of 16,300 postcards on the occasion of the 163rd anniversary of Indian Postal Day. The event also included a questionnaire about the Indian flag.

Largest Poster Awareness Campaign - Dr. Pillai designed an awareness campaign on the subject of "Beti Bachao - Beti Padhao" (Save the Girl Child - Educate the Girl Child) to achieve this record.

Largest Envelope - In tribute to the Indian Prime Minister's

"Make in India" initiative, Dr. Pillai created a 4000 square meter envelope using waste paper to achieve this record.

Attempted - **70000 Candles on a 210 kg Cake** - To celebrate the 70th Indian Independence Day, Dr. Pillai attempted to light 70,000 candles on a 210 kg cake, which was recorded in World Records India.

Attempted - **Documentary on Dhamek Stupa of Sarnath in 17 Languages** - Dr. Pillai attempted to create a documentary on the Dhamek Stupa of Sarnath, dubbing it in 17 different languages. The result of this attempt is currently awaiting confirmation from the Guinness World Records.

Dr. Pillai is skilled in teaching the Bhagavad Gita, a Hindu scripture, and is popular among young people. He has helped many young people improve their lives through his motivational teachings.

In addition to teaching, he has composed and sung numerous Sanskrit Bhajans and patriotic songs.

He has also written and directed several short films and documentaries for awareness campaigns, and has volunteered with the police in both UP and Kerala to spread awareness about various issues through videos and photography.

Incredibly, he has produced and directed over 100 documentaries about the city of Varanasi, all on his own.

He has also helped and guided more than 25 boys and girls to achieve world records through creative and innovative methods. He is a multifaceted person who uses his intellect and the blessings given to him by God to excel in various areas. He is both a teacher and a student, always learning and teaching, and is able to master any subject he comes across.

He is a selfless social activist and motivational speaker who has overcome struggles and failures to become a successful and enthusiastic individual with a rich life experience.

In addition to his work with the Bhagavad Gita, he is also an efficient Tarot card reader, Astro-Vastu consultant, and a talented singer and composer. He has sung the entire Ram Charita Manas and Bhagavad Gita in his own compositions, and has sung the phrase "Lokah Samastha Sukhino Bhavantu" in 50 different languages. He is currently working on a detailed and scientific study of Vedas, Upanishads, Puranas, and the Bhagavad Gita. He has also composed and sung the Hanuman Chalisa and Gayatri Mantra in 108 and 1008 different compositions, respectively.

Awards - Four Times Guinness World Records, Winner of Mahatma Gandhi Vishwa Shanti Puraskar, Mahatma Gandhi Global Peace Ambassador, Kashi Ratna Award, Dr. APJ Abdul Kalam Motivational Person of the Year 2017, Mother Teresa Award, Indira Gandhi Priyadarshini Award, Bharat Vikas Ratna Award, Udyog Ratna Award, Vigyan Prasar Award, Poorvanchal Ratn Samman.

Preface

The Ganges River is one of the most iconic and revered rivers in the world. Known as the Ganga in India, it is a symbol of spiritual purification, cultural heritage and a source of life for millions of people who live along its banks. This book, "The Indian River Ganges: A Cultural and Spiritual Exploration of the River Ganges" is an attempt to delve deeper into the rich history, culture, and spirituality of the Ganges.

This book is divided into 11 chapters, each exploring a different aspect of the Ganges, starting with the origins of the river, from myth to reality, followed by the role of the Ganges in Hindu religion and mythology, its significance in art, literature, and folklore, its historical perspectives, and its ecological, economic, and social importance. The book also delves into the Ganges' significance in Buddhism and Jainism, its importance in urban areas, its role in pilgrimage, and its future challenges and opportunities.

With this book, we hope to provide readers with a comprehensive understanding of the Ganges, its past, present, and future, its spiritual and cultural significance, and the challenges it faces. We also hope to inspire readers to learn more about this great river, its people, and its culture, and to appreciate its importance in shaping the history and identity of India.

We hope you enjoy reading this book, and that it leads you to a deeper understanding and appreciation of the Indian River Ganges.

I

The Origins of the Ganges: From Myth to Reality

The Ganges is one of the most revered rivers in the world, and its origins have been the subject of much myth and legend. In Hindu religion and mythology, the Ganges is seen as a goddess, born from the foot of Lord Vishnu, who descended to earth to purify the souls of the dead and give salvation to all who bathed in her waters. According to Hindu tradition, the Ganges was brought to earth by King Bhagiratha, who performed a severe penance to Lord Brahma, the Creator, to bring the Ganges down from the heavens to purify the ashes of his ancestors.

The story of King Bhagiratha's penance is one of the most popular myths associated with the Ganges. According to the legend, King Sagara of the Surya dynasty had 60,000 sons, all of whom were burned to ashes by the sage Kapila's curse. Desperate to redeem his ancestors, King Bhagiratha performed a severe penance to Lord Brahma, who was pleased with his devotion and agreed to send the Ganges to earth to purify the ashes of his ancestors. Lord Brahma then ordered Lord Vishnu to bring the Ganges down to earth, and the river descended from the heavens through the locks of Lord Shiva's hair, and thus it got the name "Ganga" from "ga" meaning lock and "anga" meaning body.

In addition to the religious and mythological origins of the Ganges, there are also scientific and geological explanations for its formation. The Ganges is formed by the confluence of the Bhagirathi and Alaknanda rivers, which originate in the glaciers of the western Himalayas. The Ganges and its tributaries have been shaped by millions of years of erosion, caused by the uplift of the Himalayas and the shifting of tectonic plates. The Ganges and its tributaries flow through a vast plain, which was formed by the depositions of sediment brought by the river over millions of years.

The Ganges is considered to be a sacred river in Hinduism and has been mentioned in many ancient texts such as the Vedas and the Puranas. It is also considered to be the most sacred river in India, and millions of Hindus travel to its banks every year to perform rituals, take a dip in its waters, and offer prayers. The Ganges is also considered to be a symbol of purity and a source of life, and its waters are believed to have healing properties.

The origins of the Ganges are steeped in myth and legend, but also have a scientific basis. The river is seen as a goddess in Hinduism and is believed to have been brought to earth by King Bhagiratha's penance. The Ganges is also formed by the confluence of the Bhagirathi and Alaknanda rivers, which originate in the glaciers of the western Himalayas. The Ganges is a sacred river, and millions of Hindus travel to its banks every year to perform rituals, take a dip in its waters, and offer prayers.

"The Ganges is not just a river, it is a
goddess, a mother, a life force, a symbol of
spiritual purification."

৪৩

II

The Ganges in Hindu Religion and Mythology

The Ganges holds a significant place in Hindu religion and mythology. It is considered to be a goddess, known as Ganga Ma, and is believed to have the power to purify the souls of the dead and give salvation to all who bathe in her waters. The Ganges is also seen as a symbol of purity and a source of life, and its waters are believed to have healing properties.

In Hindu mythology, the Ganges is said to have originated from the foot of Lord Vishnu, and was brought to earth by King Bhagiratha, who performed a severe penance to Lord Brahma, the Creator, to bring the Ganges down from the heavens to purify the ashes of his ancestors. Lord Brahma then ordered Lord Vishnu to bring the Ganges down to earth, and the river descended from the heavens through the locks of Lord Shiva's hair.

The Ganges is also associated with many other gods and goddesses in Hindu mythology. Lord Shiva is often depicted as the guardian of the Ganges and is said to reside on the mountain where the river originates. Lord Vishnu is also associated with the Ganges, and it is believed that he descended to earth in the form of the Ganges to purify the souls of the dead. The Ganges is also associated with the goddesses Parvati and Durga, who are said to reside on the banks of the river.

The Ganges is also an important part of Hindu rituals and ceremonies. Millions of Hindus travel to the banks of the Ganges every year to perform rituals, take a dip in its waters, and offer prayers. The Ganges is also a central part of the Char Dham Yatra, a pilgrimage to four sacred temples in the Indian Himalayas, which includes a dip in the Ganges at each temple.

The Ganges also holds a significant place in Hindu literature, including the Vedas and the Puranas. The river is mentioned in many ancient texts and is seen as a symbol of purification, fertility, and regeneration.

The Ganges holds a significant place in Hindu religion and mythology. It is considered to be a goddess, known as Ganga Ma, and is believed to have the power to purify the souls of the dead and give salvation to all who bathe in her waters. It is also an important part of Hindu rituals and ceremonies and holds a central place in Hindu literature.

"The Ganges is the river of India, beloved of her people, round which are interwoven her memories, her hopes and fears, her songs of triumph, her victories and her defeats." - Mark Twain

III

The Ganges as a Source of Life: Ecological and Economic Importance

The Ganges River, also known as the Ganga, is a sacred river for Hindus and one of the most important rivers in India. It originates in the western Himalayas and flows for over 1,500 miles before emptying into the Bay of Bengal. The Ganges not only plays a crucial role in the religious and cultural lives of the people who live along its banks, but it also has significant ecological and economic importance.

Ecologically, the Ganges is home to a diverse array of plant and animal life. It supports over 140 fish species, 90 amphibian species, and the endangered Ganges river dolphin. The river also provides a critical source of water for irrigation and drinking for millions of people living in the surrounding region. Additionally, the Ganges delta is a major contributor to the productivity of the Bay of Bengal, providing critical habitat for fish and other marine life.

Economically, the Ganges is an important source of income for millions of people living along its banks. It supports a thriving agricultural industry, as well as a growing tourism industry. The river is also a source of hydroelectric power, with several dams and power plants located along its course. Furthermore, the Ganges also plays a critical role in the transportation of goods and people, with numerous ports and ferry services operating along its banks.

Despite its importance, the Ganges faces a number of serious environmental challenges. Pollution from industrial and agricultural activities, as well as the rapid growth of population along its banks, has led to degradation of water quality. Additionally, over-extraction of water for irrigation and the construction of dams has led to a reduction in the flow of the river, impacting the ecosystem and the livelihoods of people dependent on it.

To preserve the ecological and economic benefits provided by the Ganges, it is important to take steps to protect and restore the river's health. This includes reducing pollution, implementing sustainable agricultural practices, and managing water resources more effectively. Additionally, the government should also invest in infrastructure and development projects that take into account the needs of the ecosystem and the people who depend on it.

The Ganges is not only a sacred river for Hindus but also a vital source of life for millions of people living in India. It plays a critical role in the ecological and economic well-being of the region and its preservation is crucial for the sustainable development of the country.

*"To bathe in the Ganges is to wash away a
lifetime of sins."*

কত

Ganges River Pilgrimage: The Significance of Char Dham Yatra

The Char Dham Yatra is a pilgrimage to four sacred temples in the Indian Himalayas, which is considered to be one of the most sacred journeys for Hindus. The temples are located in the states of Uttarakhand and Himachal Pradesh, and include the temples of Badrinath, Kedarnath, Gangotri, and Yamunotri. The journey is believed to wash away one's sins and the visit to these four temples is considered to be equivalent of visiting all the four Dhams (abodes) of Hindu god Vishnu.

The Char Dham Yatra includes a dip in the Ganges at each temple, which is considered to be a purifying and spiritual experience. The Ganges is seen as a goddess, known as

Ganga Ma, and is believed to have the power to purify the souls of the dead and give salvation to all who bathe in her waters. Taking a dip in the Ganges during the Char Dham Yatra is considered to be a way to purify one's soul and attain salvation.

The Char Dham Yatra is also a significant cultural and historical journey, as it passes through some of the most beautiful and remote regions of the Indian Himalayas. The journey includes visits to ancient temples, shrines, and monasteries, which are rich in history and cultural significance.

In addition to its spiritual and cultural significance, the Char Dham Yatra is also an important economic activity for the local communities, providing employment and income through tourism-related activities. The Char Dham Yatra also provides a significant boost to the local economy, as it attracts millions of tourists every year.

The Char Dham Yatra is a pilgrimage to four sacred temples in the Indian Himalayas, which is considered to be one of the most sacred journeys for Hindus. The journey includes a dip in the Ganges at each temple, which is considered to be a purifying and spiritual experience. It is also a significant cultural and historical journey, and an important economic activity for the local communities. The Char Dham Yatra is a unique blend of spirituality, culture, and tradition that holds a special place in the hearts of Hindus.

"The Ganges is the holiest of rivers, and to
bathe in it is to purify the body and the soul."
- Mahatma Gandhi

V

Ganges and the Cities: An Urban Perspective

The Ganges River and the cities along its banks have a unique relationship, one that is shaped by both culture and geography. From the ancient cities of Varanasi and Allahabad to the modern metropolises of Kolkata and Patna, the Ganges has played a vital role in the development and growth of these urban centers.

One of the most significant impacts of the Ganges on cities is its role as a source of water and transportation. The Ganges is one of the most important rivers in India, providing water for irrigation and drinking, as well as serving as a major transportation route for goods and people. Many cities along the Ganges have developed around ports and riverfronts, with the river serving as an integral part of the local economy.

The Ganges is also an important cultural and spiritual center for the cities along its banks. The cities of Varanasi, Allahabad, and Haridwar are considered to be among the most sacred cities in India, and are visited by millions of Hindus every year for religious and spiritual reasons. The Ganges is also an important site for the practice of Hinduism, with many temples, ashrams, and other religious institutions located along its banks.

The Ganges also plays a significant role in shaping the social and cultural fabric of the cities along its banks. The river is an important part of daily life, with many festivals and ceremonies being held in its honor. The Ganges is also an important source of inspiration for art, literature, and music.

However, the Ganges also faces significant challenges in the context of urban areas. The cities along its banks are grappling with issues such as pollution, overcrowding, and inadequate infrastructure, which have a negative impact on the river and the people who depend on it. The river also faces a growing threat from climate change, which is expected to lead to more frequent and severe floods and droughts.

The Ganges and the cities along its banks have a unique relationship, one that is shaped by both culture and geography. The Ganges plays a vital role in the development and growth of these urban centers, serving as a source of water and transportation, an important cultural and spiritual center and also shaping the social and cultural fabric of the cities, but at the same time the river faces significant challenges from pollution, overcrowding, and inadequate infrastructure, which have a negative impact on the river and the people who depend on it.

"The Ganges is not just a river, it is a
reflection of the soul of India."

೫

VI

The Ganges in Art, Literature and Folklore

The Ganges river has long been an inspiration for art, literature, and folklore in India. The river's cultural and spiritual significance, as well as its natural beauty, has been captured in various forms of art, literature, and folklore, providing a glimpse into the rich cultural heritage and traditions associated with the Ganges.

In art, the Ganges has been depicted in various forms, from traditional Indian paintings and sculptures to contemporary art. The river's natural beauty and cultural significance have been captured by artists in various mediums, including painting, sculpture, and photography. The Ganges is also an important subject in Indian miniature paintings, which depict the river's landscapes, religious and mythological stories, and daily life scenes.

In literature, the Ganges has been celebrated in poetry, fiction, and non-fiction. The river's cultural and spiritual significance is reflected in the works of many famous Indian poets, such as Rabindranath Tagore, and the Ganges is also a popular subject in Indian fiction, providing a backdrop to stories of love, adventure, and spiritual discovery. The Ganges is also the subject of many non-fiction works, including travelogues, memoirs, and historical accounts.

In folklore, the Ganges is a popular subject of folktales and legends, passed down through generations. These stories often revolve around the river's cultural and spiritual significance, and include tales of gods and goddesses, kings and queens, and common people. These stories often convey important moral and ethical values, and provide insight into the customs, beliefs, and traditions associated with the Ganges.

The Ganges river has long been an inspiration for art, literature, and folklore in India. The river's cultural and spiritual significance, as well as its natural beauty, has been captured in various forms of art, literature, and folklore, providing a glimpse into the rich cultural heritage and traditions associated with the Ganges. The Ganges has been depicted in various forms of art, celebrated in poetry and fiction and also a popular subject of folktales and legends, passed down through generations, which convey important moral and ethical values and provide insight into the customs, beliefs, and traditions associated with the Ganges.

ॐ

"The Ganges is the river of life, the river of
salvation, the river of immortality."

ॐ

VII

The Ganges in Modern Times: Challenges and Conservation Efforts

The Ganges River, also known as the Ganga, is one of the most important rivers in India, both culturally and economically. However, in recent times the Ganges has faced a number of challenges that have threatened its ecological and economic importance. These challenges include pollution, over-extraction of water, and the construction of dams. In order to preserve the Ganges, various conservation efforts have been undertaken by the government and non-governmental organizations

One of the major challenges facing the Ganges is pollution. The river is heavily polluted by industrial and agricultural waste, as well as untreated sewage. This has led to the degradation of water quality and has resulted in serious health problems for the people living along its banks. The government has taken steps to address this problem by implementing stricter regulations on industrial and agricultural activities, and by investing in sewage treatment plants. However, enforcement of these regulations and the maintenance of the treatment plants are ongoing issues.

Another major challenge facing the Ganges is the over-extraction of water for irrigation and the construction of dams. These activities have led to a reduction in the flow of the river, which has had a negative impact on the ecosystem and the livelihoods of people dependent on it. The government has been working to address this issue by implementing sustainable water management practices and by investing in irrigation infrastructure.

To conserve and protect the Ganges, the government has launched several initiatives such as the National Ganga River Basin Authority (NGRBA) in 2009, which is responsible for the conservation and rejuvenation of the Ganges and its tributaries. The Ganga Action Plan (GAP) was launched in 1985, which aimed to improve the water quality of the river by reducing pollution from industrial and municipal sources. The Namami Gange program was launched in 2014, which is an Integrated Conservation Mission with a budget of INR 20,000 crore to accomplish the twin objectives of effective abatement of pollution, conservation, and rejuvenation of the river Ganga.

In addition to government initiatives, various non-governmental organizations (NGOs) have also been working to conserve the Ganges. These organizations have been working on projects to improve water quality, protect wildlife, and promote sustainable development along the river.

The Ganges River is of great importance to the people of India, both culturally and economically. However, the river is facing a number of challenges that threaten its ecological and economic importance. The government and non-governmental organizations have taken steps to address these challenges and conserve the Ganges, but there is still much work to be done to ensure the long-term health and sustainability of the river.

"The Ganges is the river of the gods, the river
of the soul, the river of peace."

ॐ

VIII

The Ganges in the World: Influence and Impact

The Ganges river, also known as the Ganga, is not only an important river in India but also holds great significance around the world. Its cultural, spiritual, and ecological significance has had a profound influence and impact on various aspects of the world.

The Ganges is considered to be a sacred river in Hinduism, and its religious significance has been a source of inspiration for people around the world. The river is seen as a symbol of purification, fertility, and regeneration, and its waters are believed to have healing properties. The Ganges has also been a source of inspiration for art, literature, and music, and its cultural significance has been recognized around the world.

The Ganges is also an important ecological resource, and its impact on the world's environment is significant. The river and its tributaries provide water for irrigation and drinking, and its wetlands and floodplains provide important habitats for a wide variety of plant and animal species. The Ganges is also an important source of sediment, which helps to shape the landscapes of the region.

The Ganges is also an important economic resource, providing employment and income through agriculture, fishing, and tourism-related activities. The river is a major transportation route for goods and people, and the cities along its banks have developed around ports and riverfronts. The Ganges is also an important source of hydroelectric power, and its water is used for irrigation and drinking.

However, the Ganges is facing significant challenges, including pollution, over-extraction of water, and climate change. These challenges threaten the ecological, cultural, and economic resources that the Ganges provides, and their impact on the world is significant.

The Ganges river holds great significance around the world, not only in India but also globally. Its cultural, spiritual, and ecological significance has had a profound influence and impact on various aspects of the world, including religious, artistic, environmental, economic, and social. However, the river is facing significant challenges, including pollution, over-extraction of water, and climate change, which threaten the ecological, cultural, and economic resources that the Ganges provides, and their impact on the world is significant.

౩

• 39 •

"The Ganges is the river of the past, the
present, and the future."

౭ఌ

IX

Ganges and Indus Valley Civilization: A Historical Perspective

The Indus Valley Civilization, also known as the Harappan Civilization, was one of the world's earliest urban civilizations, which flourished in the northwestern region of the Indian subcontinent around 3300 BCE to 1300 BCE. The civilization was characterized by advanced city planning, monumental architecture, and sophisticated engineering, and its people were skilled in metallurgy, pottery, and textile production. The Indus Valley Civilization was also known for its sophisticated system of writing, which has not been fully deciphered yet.

The Ganges river and its tributaries, including the Indus, played a significant role in the development and decline of the Indus Valley Civilization. The civilization developed around the Indus and its tributaries, which provided water for irrigation, transportation, and communication. The civilization's cities, such as Harappa and Mohenjo-Daro, were located along the Indus and its tributaries, and the river was an important part of the civilization's economy and culture.

However, the decline of the Indus Valley Civilization is thought to have been caused, in part, by changes in the course of the Indus and other rivers. The Indus and its tributaries are known to have shifted course over time, and it is believed that the shifting river channels may have led to changes in the availability of water for irrigation, which in turn led to the decline of the civilization's agricultural economy.

The Ganges river, on the other hand, is not directly associated with the Indus Valley Civilization but it is considered to be one of the oldest rivers on Earth and the Ganges basin has been inhabited by human populations for thousands of years. The Ganges and its tributaries have also played an important role in the development of later civilizations in the region, including the Maurya, Gupta, and Mughal empires. These civilizations were characterized by significant cultural, religious, and economic achievements, and the Ganges was an important part of their economy and culture.

The Indus Valley Civilization and the Ganges river have a historical connection. The Indus Valley Civilization developed around the Indus and its tributaries, which provided water for irrigation, transportation, and communication, but the decline of the civilization is thought to have been caused, in part, by changes in the course of the Indus and other rivers. The Ganges, on the other hand, is not directly associated with the Indus Valley Civilization but it is considered to be one of the oldest rivers on Earth and the Ganges basin has been inhabited by human populations for thousands of years and has played an important role in the development of later civilizations in the region.

*All the superior religions had their growth
between the Ganga and the Euphrates*

ॐ

X

The Ganges in Buddhism and Jainism

The Ganges river holds great significance in Buddhism and Jainism, two of the major religions that originated in India. Both religions have a long history and deep connections to the Ganges, which is seen as a symbol of spiritual purification, and many important religious figures and events are associated with the river.

In Buddhism, the Ganges is associated with the life of the Buddha, who is said to have attained enlightenment while meditating under a tree near the river. The Buddha also gave several sermons and teachings on the banks of the Ganges, and many Buddhist monasteries, temples, and stupas were built along the river.

The Ganges also holds great significance in Jainism, which

also originated in India. Jainism is a religion that emphasizes non-violence and spiritual purification, and the river is seen as a symbol of spiritual purification. Many Jain monasteries, temples, and shrines are located along the banks of the Ganges, and the river is also an important site for Jain pilgrimage.

In both Buddhism and Jainism, the act of taking a dip in the Ganges is considered to be a purifying act, which can wash away one's sins and bring spiritual benefits. The river is also seen as a source of spiritual inspiration, and many religious texts, such as the Jain Agamas, and Buddhist sutras, mention the Ganges.

The Ganges river holds great significance in Buddhism and Jainism, two of the major religions that originated in India. Both religions have a long history and deep connections to the Ganges, which is seen as a symbol of spiritual purification, many important religious figures and events are associated with the river. The Ganges also holds significance in both Buddhism and Jainism in terms of pilgrimage and spiritual purification, and it is an important site for many religious monasteries, temples, and shrines.

The place of pilgrimage is Ganga only, and rivers are only a group of pure water.

XI

The Future of the Ganges: Challenges and Opportunities

The Ganges river, also known as the Ganga, is one of the most important rivers in India, providing water for irrigation, drinking, and transportation for millions of people. However, the river is facing a range of challenges that threaten its ecological, cultural, and economic resources.

One of the most significant challenges facing the Ganges is pollution. The river is heavily polluted with industrial, agricultural, and domestic waste, which poses a threat to human health and the environment. The pollution also affects the river's ability to support aquatic life and impacts the tourism and fishing industries.

Another major challenge is the over-extraction of water.

The Ganges is heavily over-exploited for irrigation and drinking water, which leads to reduced flows and increased water stress. This also affects the river's ability to support aquatic life and contributes to the decline of the Ganges' ecological health.

Climate change is also a significant threat to the Ganges, which is expected to lead to more frequent and severe floods and droughts. This will have a negative impact on the river's ecological health and the people who depend on it for their livelihoods.

Despite these challenges, the Ganges also presents significant opportunities for sustainable development. The river has the potential to support a wide range of economic activities, such as tourism, hydropower, and fisheries. There are also opportunities to improve the management of the river's resources through conservation, restoration, and sustainable development initiatives.

The Ganges river is facing a range of challenges that threaten its ecological, cultural, and economic resources, including pollution, over-extraction of water, and climate change. Despite these challenges, the Ganges also presents significant opportunities for sustainable development. Addressing these challenges and seizing these opportunities will require a collaborative effort involving governments, communities, and other stakeholders.

Other Books Of The Author

1. The Moments When I Met God
2. Kashiyile Theertha Pathangal
3. GURU GYAN VANI
4. Abhiprerak Gita
5. ASSI SE JAIN GHAT TAK
6. Hopelessness of Arjuna
7. The Soul and It's True Nature
8. Sense of Action (Karma)
9. Action through Wisdom
10. Action through Wisdom
11. THEORY AND PRACTICAL OF EVERY ACTION
12. LOGICAL UNDERSTANDING OF THE SUPREME
13. THE IMPERISHABLE SUPREME
14. Yatra Nishadraj se Hanuman Ghat Tak
15. Yatra Karnatak Ghat se Raja Ghat Tak
16. Yatra Pandey Ghat se Prayagraj Ghat Tak
17. Yatra Ranjendra Prasad Ghat se Dattatreya Ghat Tak
18. YaatraSindhiya Ghat se Gwaliar Ghat Tak
19. Yatra Mangala Gauri Ghat se Hanuman Gadhi Ghat Tak
20. Yatra Gaay Ghat Se Nishad Ghat Tak
21. MAA GANGA, GHATEN EVM UTSAV
22. Ganga Arti Dev Deepavali evam Any Utsav
23. Potentials of Digitalized India
24. VEDIC CONSCIOUSNESS
25. A Brief Introduction to Vedic Science
26. Kashi ke Barah Jyotirling
27. IMPACT OF MOTIVATION
28. Let's have a Milky Way Journey
29. Color Therapy in a Nutshell

30. Rigveda in a Nutshell
31. Yajurveda in a Nutshell
32. Samveda in a Nutshell
33. Atharva Veda in a Nutshell
34. Ayushman Bhava - Ayurveda
35. Srimad Bhagavad Gita and Upanishad Connection
36. Srimad Bhagavad Gita - an attempt to summarize each chapter.
37. Facts and Impact of Nakshatra
38. Astro Gems - NAVARATNA
39. Ekadashi - A Concise Overview
40. A Concise View of Hanuman Chalisa
41. Inspirational Gita
42. Nakshatraranyam
43. Summary of 18 Mahapuranas
44. Synopsis of 18 Upa Puranas
45. Rigvediya Upanishads
46. Shukla Yajurvediya Upanishads
47. Krishna Yajurvediya Upanishads
48. Samavediya Upanishads
49. Atharvavediya Upanishads
50. The Seven Great Sages
51. From Rocket Scientist to President Dr. APJ Abdul Kalam
52. The Visionary's Voice - Quotes of Dr. APJ Abdul Kalam
53. The Wisdom of Swami Vivekananda: Insights and Inspiration from a Legendary Spiritual Teacher
54. Ayurvedic Remedies from the Garden
55. Sages and Seers
56. Rising Strong – Motivational Stories of Women
57. Beyond Flames -Mystery stories of Funeral Ghat Manikarnika
58. The Origins of Tulsi: A Look at the Mythological Roots of the Plant"

59. The Holistic Cow: A Look at the Physical, Spiritual, and Cultural Importance of Cows in India
60. Arts of Healing
61. Exploring the Divine
62. Understanding Five Elements
63. The Etymology of Ram
64. Symbols of India
65. Voice of Change (About Speeches of Great Men)
66. She Speaks (About Speeches of Great Women)
67. Patriotism on Celluloid – Brief About Patriotic Films
68. The Music of Motivation: A Brief Guide to Inspirational Film Songs
69. Unlocking the Secrets of the Dashopanishads
70. A Cultural Mosaic
71. Ancient Traditions, Modern Minds
72. Ecos of Ancient Wisdom
73. Beneath the Surface
74. From Temples to Ashrams
75. Sages of the Subcontinent
76. The Art of Healling (Ayurveda, Yoga & Naturopathy)
77. Indian Kitchen
78. The Festivals of India
79. The Indian Epics Retold
80. The Power of Mantras

CONTACT

DR. JAGADEESH PILLAI

PhD in Vedic Science

Four Times Guinness World Record Holder

Winner of Mahatma Gandhi Vishwa Shanti Puraskar and
Global Peace Ambassador

Gemology, Astro & Vastu Consultant - Spiritual Counselor

Consultant for designing World Record Ideas

Efficient Tarot Card Reader

9839093003

myrichindia@gmail.com

drjagadeeshpillai@facebook

drjagadeeshpillai@instagram

jagadeeshpillai@youtube

www. JAGADEESHPILLAI.com

|| LOKAHA SAMASTHAHA SUKHINO BHAVANTU ||

• 61 •

www.ingramcontent.com/pod-product-compliance
Lightning Source LLC
Chambersburg PA
CBHW031329130726
47988CB00007B/3050